Great Achievements of the Democratic Party

A detailed outline of everything the Democrats have achieved.

N/A

N/A

N/A

N/A

No Records Found

N/A

N/A

N/A

N/A

N/A

N/A